RICH NUGGETS

A Daily Dose of Inspiration
to Jump-start Your Day

Dr. Richard Osibanjo

i

Copyright © 2023 by Dr. Richard Osibanjo

All rights reserved.

No part of this publication may be reproduced, distributed, or transmitted in any form or by any means, including photocopying, recording, or other electronic or mechanical methods, without the prior written permission of the publisher, except as permitted by U.S. copyright law. For permission requests, contact richardosibanjo.com.

To you— live your best life and make maximum impact

Introduction

Experience a daily dose of success and life-changing inspiration with Rich Nuggets! Dr. Richard Osibanjo's powerful quotes are crafted to help you unlock your full potential and make a meaningful impact. Dr. Osibanjo's professional journey in analytical chemistry and process engineering led to a compelling interest in the chemistry of people, leadership, and organizations. Embark on a journey that took him across the globe, ultimately leading him to become a renowned expert in transformational and purpose-driven leadership.

With over two decades of experience working with leaders and managers of medium and large-scale organizations, his extraordinary career journey has equipped him with the knowledge and insights to empower individuals to become influential leaders. Get inspired to live a more fulfilling and fruitful life by reading and contemplating these quotes.

Rich Nuggets covers many life and business topics, including leadership, relationships, mindset, goal setting, organizational growth, employee engagement, and more.

RICH NUGGETS

This book is easy to read. Experience the entire book in one sitting or savor a daily dose of Rich Nuggets. You'll want to read it more than once, whichever method you choose. Don't just read them; pause, reflect, and take action on what you've absorbed. Remember, knowledge is only powerful when it is applied. So, share your valuable insights with colleagues and loved ones.

Discover fresh inspiration and renewed motivation each time you pick it up. I hope these Rich Nuggets bring you and everyone you encounter great success and happiness.

RICH NUGGETS

A Daily Dose of Inspiration to Jump-start Your Day

RICH NUGGETS

Day 1 of 365

Due to drought, plant leaves turn yellow and then brown. These early and visible symptoms trigger remediation strategies that can restore them to health. For people, they are not so visible and are often ignored. The world needs you, so prioritize your mental health.

Dr. Richard Osibanjo

Day 2 of 365

Are you feeling burnt out lately? Like your computer, you have three options at your fingertips: standby, turn off, or restart. With the restart option, you can take a moment to pause, reflect, and then take action. What would this look like for you?

Dr. Richard Osibanjo

RICH NUGGETS

Day 3 of 365

What you see, hear, feel, say, and think about influences the outcomes you see in your life. If you are unhappy with the way your life is going, you may need to change your environment.

Dr. Richard Osibanjo

Day 4 of 365

You can't tell if a roof leaks from the outside. So, the accurate measure of an organization's culture and leadership is not from its website but from how they treat their employees.

Dr. Richard Osibanjo

RICH NUGGETS

Day 5 of 365

Your wardrobe can tell me about your style, but your library can tell me about your future. Never become so busy that you stop learning.

Dr. Richard Osibanjo

Day 6 of 365

A dollar bill has value despite being old, worn, or crumpled. Similarly, you are valuable regardless of what people say or what life throws at you.

Dr. Richard Osibanjo

RICH NUGGETS

Day 7 of 365

In 1886, a pharmacist and veteran, John Pemberton, embarked on a quest to find relief for his chronic pains. Little did he know his journey would lead him to create Coca-Cola, the iconic beverage we all know and love today. Life doesn't always go how you intend, but for every detour, there is a lesson or an opportunity to be grasped.

Dr. Richard Osibanjo

Weekly reflection activity

How do these quotes apply to my life or current situation?

RICH NUGGETS

Day 8 of 365

Even though stars are always present, they are only visible at night. Your job is to find the place, project, or people that let the star in you shine.

Dr. Richard Osibanjo

Day 9 of 365

There is always room for improvement or mediocrity. You can't be in both rooms at once, so choose wisely.

Dr. Richard Osibanjo

RICH NUGGETS

Day 10 of 365

Try it again. You may need to change your strategy, but quitting is not an option.

Dr. Richard Osibanjo

Day 11 of 365

A laser beam is powerful because it has only one wavelength. You can't do everything. Focus on your focus.

Dr. Richard Osibanjo

RICH NUGGETS

Day 12 of 365

If someone doesn't recognize the value of diamonds when they see one, that's on them, not you.

Dr. Richard Osibanjo

Day 13 of 365

Getting the word out about who you are and what you do is essential. If you don't, the opinions of others will determine your value. Control your narrative because your reality may differ from others.

Dr. Richard Osibanjo

RICH NUGGETS

Day 14 of 365

With so many distractions, it's important to take time each day to pause, reflect, and act. In quietness and confidence lies your strength.

Dr. Richard Osibanjo

Weekly reflection activity

Is there anything about these quotes that challenge my beliefs or assumptions?

RICH NUGGETS

Day 15 of 365

Today's solutions are tomorrow's museum pieces. You need to reinvent yourself if you want to remain relevant.

Dr. Richard Osibanjo

Day 16 of 365

What causes are you passionate about? You are the solution to your national, regional, and local problems. Time is running out; the world needs you.

Dr. Richard Osibanjo

RICH NUGGETS

Day 17 of 365

Truth and a positive attitude are two things that defy gravity.

Dr. Richard Osibanjo

Day 18 of 365

What is your dream? Are you pursuing it? If not, what is getting in the way? What are you going to do about it?

Dr. Richard Osibanjo

RICH NUGGETS

Day 19 of 365

When politics takes the front row in your organization, innovation, productivity and morale take the back seats.

Dr. Richard Osibanjo

Day 20 of 365

It is not worth compromising your values to fit in. Potential is discerned, not proven. There are people out there who value your uniqueness. Go out and find them.

Dr. Richard Osibanjo

RICH NUGGETS

Day 21 of 365

When you take your team for granted, innovation becomes grounded. Are you speaking your team's language?

Dr. Richard Osibanjo

Weekly reflection activity

How can you step outside your comfort zone to grow?

RICH NUGGETS

Day 22 of 365

Insecure leaders want to be the smartest people in the room.

Dr. Richard Osibanjo

Day 23 of 365

Trust is cumulative. Confidence in leadership means believing in the strategy, organizational capabilities, processes, systems, culture, and integrity of leaders. What areas do you need to strengthen to foster a high-trust organization?

Dr. Richard Osibanjo

RICH NUGGETS

Day 24 of 365

Messengers bring only good news in a low-trust environment. The market delivers the surprise news.

Dr. Richard Osibanjo

Day 25 of 365

Are you unconsciously living in a leadership bubble? To escape, you must actively seek out people who think and act differently from you.

Dr. Richard Osibanjo

RICH NUGGETS

Day 26 of 365

Betty White was at the top of her game until she passed away at the age of 99. She is living proof that skills might become obsolete, but a person's natural qualities and abilities do not expire. Like Betty, believe and invest in your gifts.

Dr. Richard Osibanjo

Day 27 of 365

Vulnerability is the down payment for building trust.

Dr. Richard Osibanjo

RICH NUGGETS

Day 28 of 365

No one truly understands what you are going through or how you feel. So, expressing your needs and seeking support are essential to prevent a breakdown.

Dr. Richard Osibanjo

Weekly reflection activity

How can I put these quotes into practice today?

_____
_____
_____
_____
_____
_____
_____
_____
_____
_____
_____
_____
_____
_____
_____

RICH NUGGETS

Day 29 of 365

A boss commands.
A leader inspires.

Dr. Richard Osibanjo

Day 30 of 365

Wine grows finer with age when stored at the right temperature. Under the wrong storage conditions, it ages twice as fast. What environment are you fostering on your team?

Dr. Richard Osibanjo

RICH NUGGETS

Day 31 of 365

Do you crack like an egg or bounce like a ball during challenging times? Your attitude is the differentiator.

Dr. Richard Osibanjo

Day 32 of 365

People's emotions are like butterflies, so no one can always make you happy. Happiness is a gift you share with others, not derive from them.

Dr. Richard Osibanjo

RICH NUGGETS

Day 33 of 365

Give your employees something they can't find anywhere else, and they will keep coming back.

Dr. Richard Osibanjo

Day 34 of 365

Remember, employers can always find someone else with your skill set, but there is only one of you. So, protect your mental health at all costs.

Dr. Richard Osibanjo

RICH NUGGETS

Day 35 of 365

A person unwilling to solicit or acknowledge feedback is analogous to a vehicle that has no side or rearview mirrors. A vehicle in such poor condition should not be driven on public roads. Requesting feedback is an essential component of your growth strategy.

Dr. Richard Osibanjo

Weekly reflection activity

Is there anything about these quotes that challenge my beliefs or assumptions?

_____

_____

_____

_____

_____

_____

_____

_____

_____

_____

_____

_____

_____

_____

RICH NUGGETS

Day 36 of 365

Love transcends thoughts and words. What does your love look like in action in your community?

Dr. Richard Osibanjo

Day 37 of 365

Some people remind you of your limitations, while others remind you of your potential. Who you listen to will determine your future.

Dr. Richard Osibanjo

RICH NUGGETS

Day 38 of 365

There is a leadership wrestle between the person you are today and the person you want to become. Focus on the bigger picture to get the upper hand.

Dr. Richard Osibanjo

Day 39 of 365

People join an organization because of its reputation. They stay because of the character (culture) and exit when the reputation and culture are not aligned.

Dr. Richard Osibanjo

RICH NUGGETS

Day 40 of 365

The degree of repetition is what distinguishes errors from incompetence.

Dr. Richard Osibanjo

Day 41 of 365

Understanding your purpose is key to doing meaningful work and leaning into your authentic power. Purpose is the new paycheck.

Dr. Richard Osibanjo

RICH NUGGETS

Day 42 of 365

The longevity of a business is not dependent on having cutting-edge technology or being ahead of the curve in research and development. A company's potential is determined by how much it invests in its people.

Dr. Richard Osibanjo

Weekly reflection activity

How do these quotes apply to my life or current situation?

RICH NUGGETS

Day 43 of 365

Before you criticize, show that you care. This way, you capture both the person's attention and admiration.

Dr. Richard Osibanjo

Day 44 of 365

The taste of change can vary from sour to pleasant. It depends on whether you are responding to it or resisting it.

Dr. Richard Osibanjo

RICH NUGGETS

Day 45 of 365

You cannot force anyone to love you; you shouldn't need to. Your true friends will stay with you, rain or shine.

Dr. Richard Osibanjo

Day 46 of 365

The harder a ball strikes the ground, the higher it bounces. Likewise, your attitude can turn a setback into a comeback.

Dr. Richard Osibanjo

RICH NUGGETS

Day 47 of 365

People do not place big bets on strangers. So, to achieve your goals and make a difference, you must cultivate meaningful relationships.

Dr. Richard Osibanjo

Day 48 of 365

Rejecting constructive criticism is the same as choosing to be average.

Dr. Richard Osibanjo

RICH NUGGETS

Day 49 of 365

Trust is cumulative. Confidence in leadership includes trusting the strategy, capabilities, processes, systems, competence, and character of leaders in the organization.

Dr. Richard Osibanjo

Weekly reflection activity

What insights or wisdom can I gain from these quotes?

_____

_____

_____

_____

_____

_____

_____

_____

_____

_____

_____

_____

_____

_____

RICH NUGGETS

Day 50 of 365

The expectation dilemma: You are disappointed when others don't meet your expectations. However, you don't want to live by others' standards. So, have high expectations for yourself. For others, expect nothing.

Dr. Richard Osibanjo

Day 51 of 365

Don't be the know-it-all that can't be taught new tricks. Be the curious one.

Dr. Richard Osibanjo

RICH NUGGETS

Day 52 of 365

Past performance is not always a predictor of future behavior. Your attitude is the differentiator. Thomas Edison's teacher told him he wouldn't go far in life. He died with more than a thousand patents.

Dr. Richard Osibanjo

Day 53 of 365

A leader seeks unity, not uniformity.

Dr. Richard Osibanjo

RICH NUGGETS

Day 54 of 365

A fixed mindset is a liability on high-performing teams.

Dr. Richard Osibanjo

Day 55 of 365

It will pass. Your best days are ahead of you. You have come too far to give up now.

Dr. Richard Osibanjo

RICH NUGGETS

Day 57 of 365

No one achieves success on their own. When you say you are self-made, you hide all the people who gave you opportunities to succeed.

Dr. Richard Osibanjo

Day 58 of 365

Remember that people do things based on their interests, not yours. Consequently, if truth-tellers fear getting in trouble, they will not speak up.

Dr. Richard Osibanjo

RICH NUGGETS

Day 59 of 365

Are you living the life you imagined or fulfilling the expectations of others? It's time to get off script. You are the change that the world needs.

Dr. Richard Osibanjo

Day 60 of 365

Thriving relationships are not like crutches. They are like wings that carry both of you to a higher level.

Dr. Richard Osibanjo

RICH NUGGETS

Day 61 of 365

Today is the day to say goodbye to beliefs or stories that no longer serve you.

Dr. Richard Osibanjo

Day 62 of 365

Do not let anyone look down on your ideas because of your level of experience. Isaac Newton was a student when he discovered the Laws of Motion. Like Newton, place a big bet on yourself. You have what it takes to make a difference.

Dr. Richard Osibanjo

RICH NUGGETS

Day 63 of 365

Managers are the secret weapon to unleash your organization's potential. Welcome their feedback, invite them to the leadership table, recognize their contributions, and prioritize their growth and development.

Dr. Richard Osibanjo

Weekly reflection activity

How do you remind yourself that you're enough?

RICH NUGGETS

Day 64 of 365

You are not a general-use product, so not everyone will value what you bring to the table. Also, remember that not everyone has good taste.

Dr. Richard Osibanjo

Day 65 of 365

Leaders who inspire their employees to give their discretionary energy cultivate high-trust environments.

Dr. Richard Osibanjo

RICH NUGGETS

Day 66 of 365

The purpose of a mailbox is to receive your mail. What is your purpose? Can you state it succinctly?

Dr. Richard Osibanjo

Day 67 of 365

Living your purpose is like having a unique license plate number; it helps you stand out from the crowd.

Dr. Richard Osibanjo

RICH NUGGETS

Day 68 of 365

Confession of the Day:
I am not an accident.
I am not an afterthought.
I am a person of value.
I'm going to make a difference.

Dr. Richard Osibanjo

Day 69 of 365

Who should take the first step toward reconciliation? I think it should be the stronger person.

Dr. Richard Osibanjo

RICH NUGGETS

Day 70 of 365

It's natural to put on a coat when it's cold and take it off when it's warm. Similarly, your organization's culture influences the behaviors of employees. If you want to accelerate results, start by fostering a culture that drives the right actions.

Dr. Richard Osibanjo

Weekly reflection activity

How do these quotes apply to my life or current situation?

_____

_____

_____

_____

_____

_____

_____

_____

_____

_____

_____

_____

_____

_____

_____

RICH NUGGETS

Day 71 of 365

Teammates who act like weeds contribute little to the team—they take more than they give. To become a valuable member of your team, look for ways to give.

Dr. Richard Osibanjo

Day 72 of 365

You cannot tell if an orange is sweet or sour without tasting it. Equally, don't pass judgment on someone before giving them a chance to reveal themselves.

Dr. Richard Osibanjo

RICH NUGGETS

Day 73 of 365

Life is not static. Where you are now is not always where you are going to be. Who you are now is not always who you are going to be.

Dr. Richard Osibanjo

Day 74 of 365

Stay true to who you are;
no one prefers an immitation.

Dr. Richard Osibanjo

RICH NUGGETS

Day 75 of 365

To get the best out of your mobile devices, you must charge them regularly. Similarly, you must schedule time to unwind, refuel, and recharge to maintain peak performance.

Dr. Richard Osibanjo

Day 76 of 365

When you live and make decisions out of fear, you miss out on opportunities and deprive the world of the solutions only you can provide.

Dr. Richard Osibanjo

RICH NUGGETS

Day 77 of 365

Do you make changes because you have to or because you want to? If you change when you want to, you have choices; otherwise, you are taking a chance.

Dr. Richard Osibanjo

Weekly reflection activity

How can you step outside your comfort zone to grow?

RICH NUGGETS

Day 78 of 365

Are you in search of Rockstar talent? It's important to ask if you're creating the optimal environment to attract, retain, and motivate them.

Dr. Richard Osibanjo

Day 79 of 365

Flow in relationships is about connecting with someone who shares your energy. If matching someone else's energy doesn't serve your highest good, it's time to let go and move forward.

Dr. Richard Osibanjo

RICH NUGGETS

Day 80 of 365

Employers can buy talent, but they have to earn your respect. Walk away gracefully when it's missing in a negotiation conversation.

Dr. Richard Osibanjo

Day 81 of 365

When a metal is exposed to a magnet, it begins to behave like one. Similarly, you will become like those with whom you associate. Choose wisely.

Dr. Richard Osibanjo

RICH NUGGETS

Day 82 of 365

Clinging to the past is like keeping your fingers on hot iron; it will hurt you. If you want to be free, honor it, and let it go. What pain are you still holding onto?

Dr. Richard Osibanjo

Day 83 of 365

Never give up! Remember your success is the best response for anyone who has told you that you are nothing, have nothing, and will be nothing.

Dr. Richard Osibanjo

RICH NUGGETS

Day 84 of 365

My manager once asked me, "What can I do to help you succeed in this company?" That was a defining moment. What memorable experiences will you create for your team today?

Dr. Richard Osibanjo

Weekly reflection activity

How can I use these quotes as inspiration or motivation in my life?

_____

_____

_____

_____

_____

_____

_____

_____

_____

_____

_____

_____

_____

RICH NUGGETS

Day 85 of 365

Some people have bad taste. Remember that the next time you feel rejected.

Dr. Richard Osibanjo

Day 86 of 365

David would have remained a shepherd in Israel without Goliath. Your Goliaths allow you to bounce or break when the going gets tough. Look out for the opportunities because you are coming out on top.

Dr. Richard Osibanjo

RICH NUGGETS

Day 87 of 365

A poison kills, harms, or slows biological activity, whereas a catalyst accelerates a significant change or action. Your words have the same impact. Are your comments beneficial or detrimental to others?

Dr. Richard Osibanjo

Day 88 of 365

If you genuinely care about diversity, equity, and inclusion, you must be willing to initiate difficult conversations. With love and good intentions, you always win.

Dr. Richard Osibanjo

RICH NUGGETS

Day 89 of 365

Your success is waiting on the other side of your fears. What types of risks are you willing to take?

Dr. Richard Osibanjo

Day 90 of 365

You are the solution, not the problem.

Dr. Richard Osibanjo

RICH NUGGETS

Fishes have streamlined bodies for swimming. Birds are born with the ability to fly. Monkeys have flexible bone structures that help them climb trees. Similarly, you have everything you need to be successful in life.

Dr. Richard Osibanjo

Weekly reflection activity

Is there anything about these quotes that challenge my beliefs or assumptions?

RICH NUGGETS

Day 92 of 365

The most significant letter in the alphabet of life, from A to Z, is Y. When purpose is known, success is inevitable.

Dr. Richard Osibanjo

Day 93 of 365

Your title or position is like a mask. Before people can trust you, they must know who you are.

Dr. Richard Osibanjo

RICH NUGGETS

Day 98 of 365

Do you want to find a solution or make a point? The outcome of your feedback session will depend on how people perceive your intentions. So be clear about your goal.

Dr. Richard Osibanjo

Weekly reflection activity

How can I apply the message of these quotes in my interactions with others?

RICH NUGGETS

Day 99 of 365

The actions you take today will lead to change tomorrow.

Dr. Richard Osibanjo

Day 100 of 365

Grapes are crushed to make wine. Olives are pressed to release oil. Similarly, trying times are an opportunity to tap into your inner strength and unleash your potential.

Dr. Richard Osibanjo

RICH NUGGETS

Day 101 of 365

Lasting change is an outer expression of an inner transformation.

Dr. Richard Osibanjo

Day 102 of 365

The first person you must reconcile with on your journey to freedom is yourself. Do not let a bad experience change the course of your life.

Dr. Richard Osibanjo

RICH NUGGETS

Day 103 of 365

If you 'care enough' about a person, your desire to give constructive feedback should be greater than your fear of hurting their feelings or ending the relationship.

— Dr. Richard Osibanjo

Day 104 of 365

Knives cannot sharpen themselves. Similarly, you can't grow by yourself; you need other people in your life to do so.

— Dr. Richard Osibanjo

RICH NUGGETS

Day 105 of 365

Since the Covid-19 pandemic, employees have prioritized meaningful work over finding dream jobs. Leaders who want to win the 'war for talent' will create workplaces where employees can find purpose in their careers.

Dr. Richard Osibanjo

Weekly reflection activity

How do you shift your mindset if it isn't working for you?

RICH NUGGETS

Day 106 of 365

No matter where you are now, getting to your next destination begins with one step.
If you want to walk far, get a coach.

Dr. Richard Osibanjo

Day 107 of 365

You name a fruit tree after its fruit. Similarly, you know people by their actions, not their words.

Dr. Richard Osibanjo

RICH NUGGETS

Day 108 of 365

People who believe they 'know-it-all' are correct. It just means they know very little, which is why they believe they know everything.

Dr. Richard Osibanjo

Day 109 of 365

The first debt you must pay is to believe in and love yourself.

Dr. Richard Osibanjo

RICH NUGGETS

Day 110 of 365

During difficult times, be the reason someone smiles today.

Dr. Richard Osibanjo

Day 111 of 365

When trying to solve a problem, keep the 80/20 rule in mind. Focus 80% on the solution and only 20% on the issue.

Dr. Richard Osibanjo

RICH NUGGETS

Day 112 of 365

Too many times, you let others define you by seeking their permission or validation to be yourself. You don't need anyone to treat you in a certain way to feel special. You, my friend, are one-of-a-kind and simply irreplaceable.

Dr. Richard Osibanjo

Weekly reflection activity

How do these quotes apply to my life or current situation?

_____

_____

_____

_____

_____

_____

_____

_____

_____

_____

_____

_____

_____

_____

RICH NUGGETS

Day 113 of 365

You are the lead actor in your life's story. And because you are the author, you can write your desired ending.

Dr. Richard Osibanjo

Day 114 of 365

In business, as in life, you will be exchanged if you do not change with change.

Dr. Richard Osibanjo

RICH NUGGETS

Day 115 of 365

Did you know 2 lbs of extra weight could affect a racing horse's performance? Similarly, extra weight is a no-go for top athletes. If you want to soar, let go of any excess baggage holding you back from achieving your goals.

Dr. Richard Osibanjo

Day 116 of 365

Get up.
Look up.
Move on.

Dr. Richard Osibanjo

RICH NUGGETS

Day 117 of 365

A boss tells people how to do things, but a leader lets people decide how to get things done. The latter moves the hand to action by touching the head and heart.

Dr. Richard Osibanjo

Day 118 of 365

How do you know if you have tried your best? Start by evaluating whether you are taking actions outside your comfort zone.

Dr. Richard Osibanjo

RICH NUGGETS

Day 119 of 365

The experiences and the people who have the biggest influence on your life won't always come in attractive packages. Walking away because you feel uncomfortable could end up costing you. Get curious and embrace it.

Dr. Richard Osibanjo

Weekly reflection activity

What insights or wisdom can I gain from these quotes?

RICH NUGGETS

Day 120 of 365

In a classroom, students place a premium on their performance. In a team sport, it is the collective performance that wins. Your team's culture will determine the type of success you attract.

Dr. Richard Osibanjo

Day 121 of 365

Sometimes it takes adversity to bring out your inner strength. You are stronger than you think. You've got what it takes.

Dr. Richard Osibanjo

RICH NUGGETS

Day 122 of 365

My life matters to God. He has seen me through the darkest times, and he still loves me. He is the author of my future.

Dr. Richard Osibanjo

Day 123 of 365

There is no such thing as a risk-free relationship.

Dr. Richard Osibanjo

RICH NUGGETS

Day 124 of 365

Self-care is not selfishness; an organization is only as healthy as the people leading it.

Dr. Richard Osibanjo

Day 125 of 365

Unforgiveness is like a burden. The weak carry it, but the wise let it go.

Dr. Richard Osibanjo

RICH NUGGETS

Day 126 of 365

Self-discovery is rewarding. However, you do not have to lose an eye to realize the importance of safety glasses in a lab. Accelerated growth occurs when you learn from the experiences of others.

Dr. Richard Osibanjo

Weekly reflection activity

How do these quotes apply to my life or current situation?

RICH NUGGETS

Day 127 of 365

What gets to me is entirely up to me.
I am not a slave to my emotions.

Dr. Richard Osibanjo

Day 128 of 365

You can't stop people from
talking about you, but you can
choose who you listen to.

Dr. Richard Osibanjo

RICH NUGGETS

Day 129 of 365

Life's exams can be tough, but you are tougher. You got this!

Dr. Richard Osibanjo

Day 130 of 365

Being single is not a handicap. Celebrate your life and seize the possibilities that come your way before you find or are found.

Dr. Richard Osibanjo

RICH NUGGETS

Day 131 of 365

A scar is a good reminder of the past, but learn the lessons and move on.

Dr. Richard Osibanjo

Day 132 of 365

You seek a cooler place to escape the heat. Don't isolate yourself when work-life gets rough. Get shade from a trusted friend.

Dr. Richard Osibanjo

RICH NUGGETS

Some people are born into privilege and squander it, while others are born into poverty and rise beyond it to achieve greatness. It's not where you start that matters but what you make of it.

Dr. Richard Osibanjo

Weekly reflection activity

How can I use these quotes as inspiration or motivation in my life?

_____

_____

_____

_____

_____

_____

_____

_____

_____

_____

_____

_____

_____

RICH NUGGETS

Day 134 of 365

Leaders build bridges, not walls.

Dr. Richard Osibanjo

Day 135 of 365

Always look in the direction you want to go. During downtimes, look up.

Dr. Richard Osibanjo

RICH NUGGETS

Day 136 of 365

Job = Potential - Passion - Purpose

Calling = Potential + Passion + Purpose

Dr. Richard Osibanjo

Day 137 of 365

Leadership is a team sport. Think of the untapped potential you can unlock when you partner with a coach. Great athletes have coaches. What's your excuse?

Dr. Richard Osibanjo

RICH NUGGETS

Day 138 of 365

A leader worth following is someone who can put themselves in your shoes.

Dr. Richard Osibanjo

Day 139 of 365

'US' is all we have. I need you. You need me. What unites us is stronger than what divides us. Let love lead the way.

Dr. Richard Osibanjo

RICH NUGGETS

Day 140 of 365

Barack Obama became the first black President of the United States. Mandela liberated South Africa from apartheid. There is a dream inside of you that is waiting for you to realize it. Are you going to answer the call?

Dr. Richard Osibanjo

Weekly reflection activity

What insights or wisdom can I gain from these quotes?

_____

_____

_____

_____

_____

_____

_____

_____

_____

_____

_____

_____

_____

_____

RICH NUGGETS

Day 141 of 365

I hold no grudges about what you think of me. They are your opinions, not my facts.

Dr. Richard Osibanjo

Day 142 of 365

Leaders can obtain feedback from their employees in two ways: by asking or through employee exits. Are you asking for feedback or waiting for it to be given to you?

Dr. Richard Osibanjo

RICH NUGGETS

Day 143 of 365

Mercedes-Benz, BMW, Toyota, Honda, Tesla, Ford, and other successful automobile manufacturers have a devoted fanbase. Stay true to yourself; there is an audience for you.

Dr. Richard Osibanjo

Day 144 of 365

We've all felt the sting of defeat in our lives, but with the right attitude, you can turn a mess into a message, a test into a testimony, and a trial into a triumph.

Dr. Richard Osibanjo

RICH NUGGETS

Day 145 of 365

A leader influences by prioritizing the people, which makes them care about their work.

Dr. Richard Osibanjo

Day 146 of 365

A beautiful garden requires a lot of effort to cultivate and maintain. Similarly, thriving relationships do not happen by chance; you must put in the work.

Dr. Richard Osibanjo

RICH NUGGETS

Day 147 of 365

If an individual prefers oranges to apples, that's OK. An apple trying to mimic an orange wastes time and energy. Instead, the apple should find and surround itself with apple lovers. You are enough!

Dr. Richard Osibanjo

Weekly reflection activity

How do you shift your mindset if it isn't working for you?

_____
_____
_____
_____
_____
_____
_____
_____
_____
_____
_____
_____
_____
_____

RICH NUGGETS

Day 148 of 365

Through life's journey, you will need three companions. Faith to climb mountains, courage to defeat Goliaths, and a large heart to accommodate other people.

Dr. Richard Osibanjo

Day 149 of 365

Success is not an island, and big dreams are never achieved alone. It takes a team to become successful. Who is on your winning team?

Dr. Richard Osibanjo

RICH NUGGETS

Day 150 of 365

Being the single point of failure on your team might be good for job security, but it is not a growth strategy. Leaders develop people.

Dr. Richard Osibanjo

Day 151 of 365

A culture that suppresses the expression of your voice, individuality, and originality is toxic to your growth. Great leaders make culture a top priority.

Dr. Richard Osibanjo

RICH NUGGETS

Day 152 of 365

You don't throw away a car because its battery is dead. No one is perfect. Some relationships are worth fighting for.

Dr. Richard Osibanjo

Day 153 of 365

Traveling with remarkable people is crucial if life is about the journey rather than the destination. Who should you bring on, keep, or kick off your bus?

Dr. Richard Osibanjo

RICH NUGGETS

Day 154 of 365

A blind person can describe an elephant by touching it. A smarter blind person will get other perspectives to get the full picture. A one-sided story can be true, but it is incomplete. Get curious; do not jump to conclusions.

Dr. Richard Osibanjo

Weekly reflection activity

How do these quotes apply to my life or current situation?

_____
_____
_____
_____
_____
_____
_____
_____
_____
_____
_____
_____
_____
_____
_____
_____

RICH NUGGETS

Day 155 of 365

Results − Recognitions = Resistance + Resentment + Resignations.

—Dr. Richard Osibanjo

Day 156 of 365

You are not an echo.
You are the voice of change.
You deserve to be heard.

—Dr. Richard Osibanjo

RICH NUGGETS

Day 157 of 365

If you always hold yourself back, you'll always be at the back of the line in life.

Dr. Richard Osibanjo

Day 158 of 365

What holds people back is not their degree of smartness but a lack of belief and confidence to pursue their dreams.

Dr. Richard Osibanjo

RICH NUGGETS

Day 159 of 365

You are an answer to someone's prayer.
This generation is lucky to have you.
Go out and do something wonderful.

Dr. Richard Osibanjo

Day 160 of 365

Purpose is like a steering wheel.
It helps you stay on track.

Dr. Richard Osibanjo

RICH NUGGETS

After the Covid-19 outbreak, the value proposition for employees shifted from "Work for me" to "Work with me," and leaders must adapt to remain competitive and attract talent.

Dr. Richard Osibanjo

Weekly reflection activity

What can you do today that you didn't think you could do a year ago?

RICH NUGGETS

Day 162 of 365

You are a gift to this generation.

Dr. Richard Osibanjo

Day 163 of 365

Your power comes from your gift. And a gift is only meaningful when it is given away. How are you making your gifts more accessible to others?

Dr. Richard Osibanjo

RICH NUGGETS

Day 164 of 365

Champions use the lessons of past experiences as stepping stones to enter a desired future.

Dr. Richard Osibanjo

Day 165 of 365

The backstage is for preparation, and the main stage is for performance. One day the world will shine its eyes on you. So, you better be prepared when the opportunity knocks.

Dr. Richard Osibanjo

RICH NUGGETS

Day 166 of 365

Hey Rockstar!
Go make **Amazing** happen today.

Dr. Richard Osibanjo

Day 167 of 365

Courage is going after what you want rather than settling for what you think you can get. What do you want? Go for it!

Dr. Richard Osibanjo

RICH NUGGETS

Day 168 of 365

Dear Fear,
Here is your notice.
I am no longer your slave.
I am not settling for less.
I am going for Gold.

What small steps can you take today to overcome your fears?

Dr. Richard Osibanjo

Weekly reflection activity

How can I put these quotes into practice today?

RICH NUGGETS

Day 169 of 365

Nothing will change unless you do.
Change your thinking to act differently.

Dr. Richard Osibanjo

Day 170 of 365

When you're in a toxic environment,
your strengths and skills don't matter
as much as your weaknesses.

Dr. Richard Osibanjo

RICH NUGGETS

Day 171 of 365

Only when you fail to grow from a setback can you say you've indeed failed. An opportunity for growth lies within every setback.

Dr. Richard Osibanjo

Day 172 of 365

A high-performing team is like a choir. They sing the same song and know when to sing in unison and harmony.

Dr. Richard Osibanjo

RICH NUGGETS

Day 173 of 365

Think of all the failed projects, missed deadlines, and opportunities that occur when employees opt for silence rather than risk repercussions because leadership is not accessible or doesn't listen.

Dr. Richard Osibanjo

Day 174 of 365

How can you create a culture that doesn't shoot the messenger but welcomes bad news? The growth and longevity of your business depend on it.

Dr. Richard Osibanjo

RICH NUGGETS

Day 175 of 365

Not everyone will like or support your ideas, and that is okay. Gangnam Style was a worldwide hit, despite some countries not embracing it. After its release, it was the first song on YouTube's Billion Views Club. The singer, PSY, did not try to convince his critics. He went where his fans were. Similarly, go where you are celebrated.

Dr. Richard Osibanjo

Weekly reflection activity

What do these quotes mean to me?

_____

_____

_____

_____

_____

_____

_____

_____

_____

_____

_____

_____

_____

_____

RICH NUGGETS

Day 176 of 365

Why do you think people keep talking about you? Nobody wastes time and energy on trivial matters. It is because you are a valuable person.

Dr. Richard Osibanjo

Day 177 of 365

Never base your self-esteem on other people's opinions. They can take it from you if they give it to you.

Dr. Richard Osibanjo

RICH NUGGETS

Day 178 of 365

The truth isn't always pleasant to hear. Like taking medicine, it will make you better, not bitter.

Dr. Richard Osibanjo

Day 179 of 365

It's in your DNA to succeed. You successfully fertilized an egg while facing off against 200,000,000 other sperm. Don't ever doubt your abilities or strength. You've won before and you can do it again.

Dr. Richard Osibanjo

RICH NUGGETS

Day 180 of 365

Don't let the events of your past define the rest of your life. Your future is like a blank sheet of paper. What would you like to write about?

Dr. Richard Osibanjo

Day 181 of 365

Potential is discerned, not proven. Choose wisely whose canopy you stay under. Do not settle for less. You are destined for great things.

Dr. Richard Osibanjo

RICH NUGGETS

Day 182 of 365

A SMILE
Is good for you
Looks good on you
Makes you feel good
Makes others feel great
Turns strangers into friends
Brings communities together
Restores broken relationships
And, best of all, It is free
You've got a beautiful
smile, share it today.

Dr. Richard Osibanjo

Weekly reflection activity

What insights or wisdom can I gain from these quotes?

_____
_____
_____
_____
_____
_____
_____
_____
_____
_____
_____
_____
_____

RICH NUGGETS

Day 183 of 365

When your anxiety increases, the worst of you shows up. Pause, reflect, and get back in the game. You got this!

Dr. Richard Osibanjo

Day 184 of 365

Ignoring the elephant in the room will not solve the problem. In fact, the elephant will destroy more items the longer it is allowed to roam. Whatever you refuse to confront never goes away.

Dr. Richard Osibanjo

RICH NUGGETS

Day 185 of 365

Leadership is ultimately about people. To become a leader worth following, learn how to connect and build meaningful relationships. Anything else is putting the cart before the horse.

Dr. Richard Osibanjo

Day 186 of 365

Managers are the key to engaging and energizing the workforce. Happy managers make happy employees.

Dr. Richard Osibanjo

RICH NUGGETS

Day 187 of 365

Are you waiting for someone's approval to start pursuing your dreams? The only person's opinion that should matter above anyone else is yours.

Dr. Richard Osibanjo

Day 188 of 365

Roses are beautiful in vases but don't thrive in them. The same is true of us: when we are cut off from our source, we feel a void that no one or material possessions can fill.

Dr. Richard Osibanjo

RICH NUGGETS

Day 189 of 365

Leave your past behind and embrace your future. Like the ever-changing flow of a river, you too can transform into the person you've always dreamed of becoming. Your best days are yet to come. Keep pushing forward, and never give up on your dreams!

Dennis Skinner

Weekly reflection activity

How can you step outside your comfort zone to grow?

_____

_____

_____

_____

_____

_____

_____

_____

_____

_____

_____

_____

_____

RICH NUGGETS

Day 190 of 365

Consider what you are thinking about. Your thoughts ultimately become your reality. You cannot feature in a future you can not picture.

Dr. Richard Osibanjo

Day 191 of 365

Leadership is not about getting a spot at the top. Instead, it is about paving the way for others to achieve their goals. Helping others succeed will lead to your own success.

Dr. Richard Osibanjo

RICH NUGGETS

Day 192 of 365

Ultimately, you must decide which is worse: the regret of not trying or the risk of pursuing your dreams

Dr. Richard Osibanjo

Day 193 of 365

Your options are limited only by the risks you are willing to take.

Dr. Richard Osibanjo

RICH NUGGETS

Day 194 of 365

What is possible? The answer to that question is limited only by your imagination. Change your thoughts, they will change your life.

Dr. Richard Osibanjo

Day 195 of 365

Don't give your power away. Nobody has the final say over your future. You decide whether to win or lose.

Dr. Richard Osibanjo

RICH NUGGETS

Day 196 of 365

Isaac Newton asked why an apple fell straight down from a tree. As a result, Newton discovered the Laws of Motion. Following your curiosity can lead to surprising outcomes. What piques your interest?

Dr. Richard Osibanjo

Weekly reflection activity

How do these quotes apply to my life or current situation?

RICH NUGGETS

Day 197 of 365

An apple seed is successful if it germinates and grows into an apple tree. Similarly, realizing your full potential is the best way to evaluate your achievements.

Dr. Richard Osibanjo

Day 198 of 365

Take 'no' as a comma, not a period.

Dr. Richard Osibanjo

RICH NUGGETS

Day 199 of 365

Leadership is service.

Dr. Richard Osibanjo

Day 200 of 365

Hydrangeas need regular watering to thrive; cactus do not. It's your job to let the people in your life know where you land on that spectrum. Otherwise, they will experiment at your expense.

Dr. Richard Osibanjo

RICH NUGGETS

Day 201 of 365

Today, I canceled my mediocrity mindset subscription and signed up for the 'be your best self platform'. What mindset subscription are you going to cancel today?

— Dr. Richard Osibanjo

Day 202 of 365

You are not a gamble. You are more than a safe bet. You are the real deal. The world is waiting for you to unleash your brilliance. Go out and bless the world.

— Dr. Richard Osibanjo

RICH NUGGETS

Day 203 of 365

You are wired for connection.
Make time to cultivate
meaningful relationships.
Thriving relationships are not
sustained by convenience.
Social media is a means
to an end, not an end.

Dr. Richard Osibanjo

Weekly reflection activity

What do these quotes mean to me?

RICH NUGGETS

Day 204 of 365

What happens when you walk into a room depends on whether you are perceived as a problem or a solution.

Dr. Richard Osibanjo

Day 205 of 365

You don't need anyone's permission to bring your excellence to the table.

Dr. Richard Osibanjo

RICH NUGGETS

Day 206 of 365

Do not count yourself out before entering the ring. The worst-case scenario is that someone says no. Even if you don't succeed, you would have learned something because you tried. Give it a shot.

Dr. Richard Osibanjo

Day 207 of 365

I have no regrets, only experiences that have made me wiser and stronger.

Dr. Richard Osibanjo

RICH NUGGETS

Day 208 of 365

A rubber band is most effective when it is stretched. Similarly, surround yourself with people who are smarter than you to accelerate your growth.

Dr. Richard Osibanjo

Day 209 of 365

No one is perfect. If you are looking for the perfect leader, partner, parent, child, or colleague, you will find them in heaven. Such people don't exist on earth.

Dr. Richard Osibanjo

RICH NUGGETS

Day 210 of 365

Jeff Bezos, the founder of Amazon, leaves an empty chair at the company's most important meetings to represent the voice of the customer. In today's world, you need two chairs: one for the customer and one for your employees. Like your customers, your employees deserve to be treated with respect.

Dr. Richard Osibanjo

Weekly reflection activity

Is there anything about these quotes that challenge my beliefs or assumptions?

_____

_____

_____

_____

_____

_____

_____

_____

_____

_____

_____

_____

_____

_____

RICH NUGGETS

Day 211 of 365

If you have exhausted all options and still need to let a job or a relationship go, you are not quitting; you have just taken an exit.

Dr. Richard Osibanjo

Day 212 of 365

We are a team when your success is my success and my problems are also your problems.

Dr. Richard Osibanjo

RICH NUGGETS

Day 213 of 365

Your shyness, anxieties, or waiting for permission to be yourself are depriving the world of solutions only you can bring. Turn yourself in today, and let the world experience your amazing!

Dr. Richard Osibanjo

Day 214 of 365

Being brave is not easy, but you must embrace the discomfort to reap its benefits.

Dr. Richard Osibanjo

RICH NUGGETS

Day 215 of 365

In the same way that road signs help you reach your destination, mentors provide you with the information and guidance you need to achieve your goals. You are ultimately responsible for the decisions you make.

Dr. Richard Osibanjo

Day 216 of 365

You either fight or run when you're at your breaking point. Wisdom is knowing which to choose. If your life is in danger, run; otherwise, fight.

Dr. Richard Osibanjo

RICH NUGGETS

Day 217 of 365

Books are sold in various formats, including audio, print, and electronic, to reach a wider audience. Similarly, you should adapt your leadership style to build an inclusive environment.

Dr. Richard Osibanjo

Weekly reflection activity

How can I put these quotes into practice today?

RICH NUGGETS

Day 218 of 365

Hard Work - Heart Work = Frustration
Hard Work + Heart Work = Success

Dr. Richard Osibanjo

Day 219 of 365

Daily reminder: The primary purpose of stars is to shine. You are one!

Dr. Richard Osibanjo

RICH NUGGETS

Day 220 of 365

When the rubber hits the road, a leader takes the heat for the team.

Dr. Richard Osibanjo

Day 221 of 365

Chill out! We can take our work seriously without taking ourselves too seriously.

Dr. Richard Osibanjo

RICH NUGGETS

Day 222 of 365

What are you worth? The correct answer is priceless.

Dr. Richard Osibanjo

Day 223 of 365

The soil quality will determine a seed's chance of growing. Similarly, find an environment that encourages you to pursue your dreams and advance your career.

Dr. Richard Osibanjo

RICH NUGGETS

Day 224 of 365

We are all flawed, have blind spots, and feel inadequate somehow, which is okay. When you embrace your unique and broken aspects and seek feedback, you humanize the workplace and allow others to bring their whole selves to work.

Dr. Richard Osibanjo

Weekly reflection activity

What insights or wisdom can I gain from these quotes?

RICH NUGGETS

Day 225 of 365

Don't just focus on yourself. Be the opportunity people are looking for. Who will you open the door for today?

Dr. Richard Osibanjo

Day 226 of 365

The ideal form of recognition is not appreciation for previous accomplishments, but rather an opportunity offered based on a belief in the person's potential.

Dr. Richard Osibanjo

RICH NUGGETS

Day 227 of 365

You can turn your breaking point into a turning point if you look for the opportunities.

Dr. Richard Osibanjo

Day 228 of 365

What are you afraid to do? You just answered your next growth step.

Dr. Richard Osibanjo

RICH NUGGETS

Day 229 of 365

Your biggest competitor is not the person down the street. It's becoming better than you were yesterday.

Dr. Richard Osibanjo

Day 230 of 365

This week, let your desire to achieve your goals be greater than your fear of rejection.

Dr. Richard Osibanjo

RICH NUGGETS

Day 231 of 365

Distinguishing between exiting and quitting is important. Once a person has exhausted all possibilities, they can make an educated decision and exit. When someone quits, they still have options but see them as work.

Dr. Richard Osibanjo

Weekly reflection activity

How do these quotes apply to my life or current situation?

_____

_____

_____

_____

_____

_____

_____

_____

_____

_____

_____

_____

_____

_____

RICH NUGGETS

Day 232 of 365

Authenticity is not static; it is a journey to become a better version of yourself.

Dr. Richard Osibanjo

Day 233 of 365

Who do you want to become? Start acting like that person every day. Practice makes perfect.

Dr. Richard Osibanjo

RICH NUGGETS

Day 234 of 365

The fear of criticism is the beginning of mediocrity.

Dr. Richard Osibanjo

Day 235 of 365

Those who inflicted the pains of yesterday have no power over your future. You empower the past by ruminating over it. It is time to cut the link by letting go.

Dr. Richard Osibanjo

RICH NUGGETS

Day 236 of 365

Manufacturers recommend not mixing old and new batteries to get the utmost performance. Similarly, harboring the past contaminates the present. Let it go!

Dr. Richard Osibanjo

Day 237 of 365

Using a salt shaker prevents oversalting your food. Such is the power of self awareness; it enables you to show up in a way that adds value to your audience.

Dr. Richard Osibanjo

RICH NUGGETS

A handyperson can't be successful with just a hammer in the toolbox. Similarly, surround yourself with people who complement your strengths and weaknesses.

Dr. Richard Osibanjo

Weekly reflection activity

How do you embrace your authentic self, even if it looks different from what others expect?

RICH NUGGETS

Day 239 of 365

It is common knowledge that more than 70% of change initiatives fail. Organizations pay the price when leaders surround themselves with people who do not challenge the status quo.

Dr. Richard Osibanjo

Day 240 of 365

Every fruit has its flavor. You could never blame an apple for not tasting like a banana. Similarly, stop comparing yourself to others. Accept your individuality and express your originality.

Dr. Richard Osibanjo

RICH NUGGETS

Day 241 of 365

Organizations can only improve if their leaders work on themselves first.

Dr. Richard Osibanjo

Day 242 of 365

It requires less energy to be your authentic self. Your uniqueness is your differentiator. Stop trying to fit in.

Dr. Richard Osibanjo

RICH NUGGETS

Day 243 of 365

You attract what you celebrate. So, don't be envious of the accomplishments of others.

Dr. Richard Osibanjo

Day 244 of 365

If all else fails, try love.

Dr. Richard Osibanjo

RICH NUGGETS

Day 245 of 365

The connection gap employees experience in the post-pandemic workplace is no longer a personal issue but an organizational health challenge. To drive collaboration, leaders must be intentional about fostering meaningful connections.

Dr. Richard Osibanjo

Weekly reflection activity

How can I use these quotes as inspiration or motivation in my life?

RICH NUGGETS

Day 246 of 365

Money and material things can be lost and replaced, but the loss of a loved one is final. So, how much quality time are you devoting to your true riches?

Dr. Richard Osibanjo

Day 247 of 365

Taking the time to cultivate meaningful relationships, despite your busy schedule, is beneficial to your spiritual, emotional, and social well-being. You are wired for connection.

Dr. Richard Osibanjo

RICH NUGGETS

Day 248 of 365

Not all life's problems can be solved by having a good degree or family name. There are three things you can always count on; faith, hope, and love. The greatest of these is love.

Dr. Richard Osibanjo

Day 249 of 365

When you pursue purpose, you'll discover your best self and find meaning and fulfillment.

Dr. Richard Osibanjo

RICH NUGGETS

Day 250 of 365

Boss Lady status isn't achieved by barking orders. They conquer their fears, emotions, and doubts, emerging victorious.

Dr. Richard Osibanjo

Day 251 of 365

Nothing great is built in a day but can be brought down in one. Similarly, being a person of influence is not a permanent status. Like rent, you must keep paying to enjoy its benefits.

Dr. Richard Osibanjo

A Daily Dose of Inspiration to Jump-start Your Day

RICH NUGGETS

Day 252 of 365

When emotions are in play, logic alone won't cut it. And the same goes for using emotions to solve a problem - it just won't work. Forge ahead by first establishing a shared understanding and recognizing each individual's unique perspectives.

Dr. Richard Osibanjo

A Daily Dose of Inspiration to Jump-start Your Day

Weekly reflection activity

Is there anything about these quotes that challenge my beliefs or assumptions?

RICH NUGGETS

Day 253 of 365

Trust is the currency for doing business. A lack of trust reduces velocity and productivity and raises the cost of doing business.

Dr. Richard Osibanjo

Day 254 of 365

Fear will hold you back, but courage will move you forward. Which voice do you listen to?

Dr. Richard Osibanjo

RICH NUGGETS

Day 255 of 365

Choosing the right mentor, coach, sponsor, or manager is like purchasing a pair of shoes. It must fit and be comfortable. Find one today. Your growth and success depend on it.

Dr. Richard Osibanjo

Day 256 of 365

Be selective about the people you share your weaknesses with. Some people will write them in ink, not pencil.

Dr. Richard Osibanjo

RICH NUGGETS

Day 257 of 365

Your character is like smoke; you can't keep it in. Establish credibility by maintaining an unbroken chain of good reputation and honest behavior.

Dr. Richard Osibanjo

Day 258 of 365

Career growth isn't always vertical. It can be lateral, and in some cases, it might require you to take a step down to go up.

Dr. Richard Osibanjo

RICH NUGGETS

Day 259 of 365

At zero degree Celsius, ice starts to form. At 100 degrees Celsius, water vaporizes into steam. Similarly, identifying environments that bring out your best performance will accelerate your growth.

Dr. Richard Osibanjo

Weekly reflection activity

How can you step outside your comfort zone to grow?

RICH NUGGETS

Day 260 of 365

There is a term for those who insist on keeping possessions that are not theirs. It's the same label applied to those who hoard their abilities rather than impart them to others.

Dr. Richard Osibanjo

Day 261 of 365

Selling a Ferrari to someone who can't afford a Tesla would be unethical. Similarly, don't compromise your values. Waiting for the right person or opportunity will eventually pay off.

Dr. Richard Osibanjo

RICH NUGGETS

Day 262 of 365

Life's realities may throw you a curveball, but do not let this become an excuse to settle for less. It's not over until you win .

Dr. Richard Osibanjo

Day 263 of 365

You've got one shot at life. There are no returns, refunds, or exchanges. So, invest it wisely.

Dr. Richard Osibanjo

RICH NUGGETS

Day 264 of 365

When I was a kid, I was told curiosity kills the cat. Today, it is what creates the future. What are you curious about? What path is it leading you to?

Dr. Richard Osibanjo

Day 265 of 365

Your best friends love you for being yourself. You do not need to fit a particular description to be in their lives.

Dr. Richard Osibanjo

RICH NUGGETS

Day 266 of 365

Conversations are the foundation upon which friendships and communities are built. Feeling uncomfortable around those who don't look like you is normal. Reach out anyway. A smile, text, phone call, or email, can go a long way to show you care.

Dr. Richard Osibanjo

Weekly reflection activity

What can you do today that you didn't think you could do a year ago?

RICH NUGGETS

Day 267 of 365

When your arms are open, it is easier
to lift you up. Your vulnerability
is what makes you human.
Accept it and be proud of it.

Dr. Richard Osibanjo

Day 268 of 365

It's important to distinguish between
people who are nice to you because
of your status and who you are.
It prevents disappointment when
the position disappears.

Dr. Richard Osibanjo

RICH NUGGETS

Day 269 of 365

When you embrace who you are, you give others permission to be themselves. This is how healthy and long-lasting relationships are developed.

Dr. Richard Osibanjo

Day 270 of 365

Knowledge is only powerful when it is applied.

Dr. Richard Osibanjo

RICH NUGGETS

Day 271 of 365

You can't stay in your comfort zone and accomplish great things at the same time. To walk on water, leave the boat.

Dr. Richard Osibanjo

Day 272 of 365

Taking action is the most effective way to silence that voice in your head that says you are enough.

Dr. Richard Osibanjo

RICH NUGGETS

Day 273 of 365

J.K. Rowling's Harry Potter and the Philosopher's Stone manuscript was rejected 12 times before a publisher took a chance on her. Rejection is someone's opinion. So, doubt your doubters and have faith in your dreams.

Dr. Richard Osibanjo

Weekly reflection activity

Is there anything about these quotes that challenge my beliefs or assumptions?

_____

_____

_____

_____

_____

_____

_____

_____

_____

_____

_____

_____

_____

_____

RICH NUGGETS

Day 274 of 365

Great leaders, like iron, are forged in the heat. How can you turn your problem into a gift and an opportunity?

Dr. Richard Osibanjo

Day 275 of 365

Your ability to influence and build trusting relationships accelerates results in today's uncertain and complex environment. How healthy are your relationships with coworkers and stakeholders?

Dr. Richard Osibanjo

RICH NUGGETS

Day 276 of 365

Fishermen use baits to entice and capture fish. Similarly, your mindset is like a magnet, attracting only the people and experiences you expect.

Dr. Richard Osibanjo

Day 277 of 365

Lego bricks are designed to be broken down and rebuilt; people are not. The world needs you! So prioritize your mental health to avoid burnout and stay on top of your game.

Dr. Richard Osibanjo

RICH NUGGETS

Day 278 of 365

Great leaders connect first before they ask for a hand.

Dr. Richard Osibanjo

Day 279 of 365

These days, everyone is an influencer on social media. Remember that you can tell a tree by its fruit to help you filter out the noise.

Dr. Richard Osibanjo

RICH NUGGETS

Day 280 of 365

News Alert: Your employees and colleagues are not mind readers. So, ask what makes them feel valued and how they want to be recognized. This way, you touch their heads and hearts and move their hands to action.

Dr. Richard Osibanjo

Weekly reflection activity

How do you remind yourself that you're enough?

RICH NUGGETS

Day 281 of 365

The pursuit of purpose is what distinguishes a life that is enjoyed from one that is endured. When purpose is known, success is inevitable.

Dr. Richard Osibanjo

Day 282 of 365

What other people think of you is not your problem but theirs. The less you care what other people think, the simpler your life will be.

Dr. Richard Osibanjo

RICH NUGGETS

Day 283 of 365

Taking on more responsibility does not necessarily make you a better leader. It may exacerbate problems and cause more damage. Leadership development is a crucial component of any organization's growth strategy.

Dr. Richard Osibanjo

Day 284 of 365

Leaders lead from the front during times of uncertainty. By the side during difficulty and behind during prosperous times.

Dr. Richard Osibanjo

RICH NUGGETS

Day 285 of 365

A New Year is just a date change if you don't shift your mindset.

Dr. Richard Osibanjo

Day 286 of 365

Leaders who treat their customers like kings but their employees like tools are in for a rude awakening. Employees have found their voice and are moving towards or away from employers based on how they are valued.

Dr. Richard Osibanjo

RICH NUGGETS

Day 287 of 365

Fallen leaves add nutrients and minerals to the soil. Likewise, no experience is wasted. Even the negative ones can teach you valuable lessons that will equip you for the future.

Dr. Richard Osibanjo

Weekly reflection activity

How do these quotes apply to my life or current situation?

RICH NUGGETS

Day 288 of 365

If you have plumbing issues, you seek out a plumber. For electrical problems, you find an electrician. What comes to mind when people think about you?

Dr. Richard Osibanjo

Day 289 of 365

Nobody is responsible for your growth. It's a choice you have to make.

Dr. Richard Osibanjo

RICH NUGGETS

Day 290 of 365

The path to greatness will lead you through the valley of your fears. Don't stop. Focus on the big picture, and go ahead!

Dr. Richard Osibanjo

Day 291 of 365

You are not an afterthought.
You are the real deal.
You matter.
Make it count!

Dr. Richard Osibanjo

RICH NUGGETS

Day 292 of 365

There is no fear in love. If that's not your experience, your real friends are still out there; go and find them.

Dr. Richard Osibanjo

Day 293 of 365

Great companies make their customers' lives better. They begin by focusing on their employees. Do you treat your employees like you treat a customer?

Dr. Richard Osibanjo

RICH NUGGETS

Day 294 of 365

Employees are responsible for the products, services, and solutions that delight your customers. Unengaged employees won't innovate. How are you inspiring your employees' hearts and minds?

Dr. Richard Osibanjo

Weekly reflection activity

What do these quotes mean to me?

RICH NUGGETS

Day 295 of 365

Note to self: you have earned your spot here. So, act like it.

Dr. Richard Osibanjo

Day 296 of 365

A seed will not grow unless it is planted. Which of your ideas do you need to give attention to and take to the next level?

Dr. Richard Osibanjo

RICH NUGGETS

Day 297 of 365

Build a house where you are celebrated and a tent where you are tolerated.

Dr. Richard Osibanjo

Day 298 of 365

You do not need anyone's permission to be yourself. You've waited long enough. It's time to spread your wings and fly. No limits!

Dr. Richard Osibanjo

RICH NUGGETS

Day 299 of 365

Step outside your comfort zone: The United States did not land on the moon by pursuing low-hanging fruit.

Dr. Richard Osibanjo

Day 300 of 365

Great leaders understand that an effective strategy for winning people over to their cause is first to show an interest in theirs.

Dr. Richard Osibanjo

RICH NUGGETS

Day 301 of 365

You have heard that employees leave their managers more than the organization itself. It raises the question whether or not the corporation invests enough in its managers. After all, managers can't give what they do not have.

Dr. Richard Osibanjo

Weekly reflection activity

How do you shift your mindset if it isn't working for you?

RICH NUGGETS

Day 302 of 365

The goal of constructive feedback is to influence a change in behavior while preserving or advancing the relationship.

Dr. Richard Osibanjo

Day 303 of 365

It is not the accumulation of experience that contributes to your development; it is evaluated experience.

Dr. Richard Osibanjo

RICH NUGGETS

Day 304 of 365

A leader's first task is to establish personal credibility with the team. Anything else would be putting the cart before the horse.

Dr. Richard Osibanjo

Day 305 of 365

Trust is a whole number; not a fraction. When you don't trust someone completely, it influences your actions or inactions.

Dr. Richard Osibanjo

RICH NUGGETS

Day 306 of 365

A pencil has to be sharpened to fulfill it's purpose. Similarly, growth is the reward for embracing the pains of change.

Dr. Richard Osibanjo

Day 307 of 365

Do you have big dreams? Begin by using your influence to make a difference where you are and with the people around you.

Dr. Richard Osibanjo

RICH NUGGETS

Day 308 of 365

Don't go through life by yourself. Surround yourself with people who believe in you and recognize your potential. Finding these life partners will enrich your journey and accelerate your growth.

Dr. Richard Osibanjo

Weekly reflection activity

How can I use these quotes as inspiration or motivation in my life?

_____
_____
_____
_____
_____
_____
_____
_____
_____
_____
_____
_____
_____
_____
_____

RICH NUGGETS

Day 309 of 365

Monday mornings can be something you look forward to. The pursuit of your calling and ultimate fulfillment is non-negotiable. You don't have to settle for anything less.

Dr. Richard Osibanjo

Day 310 of 365

Reciprocity is wonderful in a relationship. Nevertheless, it is a gift, not a right. Remember that no one owes you anything.

Dr. Richard Osibanjo

RICH NUGGETS

Day 311 of 365

The pursuit of becoming one with yourself should be your life's goal. When who you are and what you do are not aligned, the result is an unfulfilled life.

Dr. Richard Osibanjo

Day 312 of 365

When your beliefs are stronger than your doubts and fears, action is the natural consequence.

Dr. Richard Osibanjo

RICH NUGGETS

Day 313 of 365

We all face rejection in some form or another. Rejection itself is not the issue, but how we respond to it. Like a Teflon pan, do not let it stick.

Dr. Richard Osibanjo

Day 314 of 365

Your authenticity sets you apart in a crowded and competitive market. So, be an original leader.

Dr. Richard Osibanjo

RICH NUGGETS

Day 315 of 365

One-sided relationships drain your energy. Please do not spend time with people who act like they are doing you a favor. Invest your time with people who recognize your value.

Dr. Richard Osibanjo

Weekly reflection activity

How can I put these quotes into practice today?

RICH NUGGETS

Day 316 of 365

As you progress in life, you will lose some relationships. Some people prefer your previous self. Forcing them to stay will end up doing more harm than good.

Dr. Richard Osibanjo

Day 317 of 365

Successful businesses and relationships are built on the premise that everyone wins.

Dr. Richard Osibanjo

RICH NUGGETS

Day 318 of 365

You are not a placeholder; you are the real deal. So, own your space, and take your place.

Dr. Richard Osibanjo

Day 319 of 365

Good friends are like blankets; they keep you warm when life gets cold.

Dr. Richard Osibanjo

RICH NUGGETS

Day 320 of 365

You become what you listen to. Who are you giving permission to speak into your life?

Dr. Richard Osibanjo

Day 321 of 365

Your thoughts generate your feelings and influence your actions. As with a TV remote, you can change the channel if you don't like what is playing.

Dr. Richard Osibanjo

RICH NUGGETS

Day 322 of 365

Think of your leadership journey as developing a product. A product goes through several iterations until it's fit for purpose. These iterations are vital to your growth because they help you learn from mistakes, missed opportunities, and failed attempts.

Dr. Richard Osibanjo

Weekly reflection activity

What insights or wisdom can I gain from these quotes?

_____

_____

_____

_____

_____

_____

_____

_____

_____

_____

_____

_____

_____

_____

A Daily Dose of Inspiration to Jump-start Your Day

RICH NUGGETS

Day 323 of 365

Like a tattoo, you leave a lasting impression wherever you go. What kind of memories do you evoke when people think of you?

Dr. Richard Osibanjo

Day 324 of 365

You are not designed to do everything. You are not for everybody. And that's okay. Focus on work that reflects who you are and what you love, and success will follow.

Dr. Richard Osibanjo

RICH NUGGETS

Day 325 of 365

A leader does not control the organization; the culture does. To transform organizations, change the culture.

Dr. Richard Osibanjo

Day 326 of 365

Your gift is your calling card. It's your job to develop it and teach people how it can add value to their lives.

Dr. Richard Osibanjo

RICH NUGGETS

Day 327 of 365

I dare you to embrace your originality and be unapologetic about your creativity. You are here for a purpose. Make it count.

Dr. Richard Osibanjo

Day 328 of 365

Your fulfillment is the accurate metric of success.

Dr. Richard Osibanjo

RICH NUGGETS

Remember that most people who succeeded were told they wouldn't. You will be in the same company as Abraham Lincoln, Barack Obama, Nelson Mandela, Oprah Winfrey, and countless others. Your persistence and belief in yourself will have the last word.

Dr. Richard Osibanjo

Weekly reflection activity

How can I apply the message of these quotes in my interactions with others?

RICH NUGGETS

Day 330 of 365

A one-size-fits-all approach to management is doomed to fail. Cactus have sharp spines and different watering needs from hydrangeas, so you must handle them differently.

Dr. Richard Osibanjo

Day 331 of 365

Do not underestimate the power of prayer to tackle daily challenges.

Dr. Richard Osibanjo

RICH NUGGETS

Day 332 of 365

Be careful about lowering your standards. What you overlook or allow is teaching others how to treat you.

Dr. Richard Osibanjo

Day 333 of 365

Bridges lead to boundless opportunities, while walls confine you to a limited perspective. Building bridges is what great leaders do best!

Dr. Richard Osibanjo

RICH NUGGETS

Day 334 of 365

Being the best doesn't guarantee that opportunities will always come to you. Promote your services to increase your chances of success.

Dr. Richard Osibanjo

Day 335 of 365

Despite contrary views, the earth didn't become flat. You're valuable regardless of what people think. The real question is, whose opinion do you believe, yours or theirs?

Dr. Richard Osibanjo

RICH NUGGETS

Day 336 of 365

Free yourself from the limitations people put on you. Louis Armstrong, one of the most influential figures in jazz, was ejected from music school because he couldn't complete the music scales. His response? "They just can't keep up with me."

Dr. Richard Osibanjo

Weekly reflection activity

Is there anything about these quotes that challenge my beliefs or assumptions?

RICH NUGGETS

Day 337 of 365

A Ferrari in a showroom is stunning, but it is designed to be driven. You are like that Ferrari when you are not maximizing your potential.

Dr. Richard Osibanjo

Day 338 of 365

Relationships with loved ones should be meaningful and the bonds stronger than a mere kitchen towel.

Dr. Richard Osibanjo

RICH NUGGETS

Day 339 of 365

If you want your garden to thrive, space out the seeds before planting to prevent them from choking each other. Similarly, relationships thrive when you give each other room to grow.

Dr. Richard Osibanjo

Day 340 of 365

There is no single recipe for a happy relationship, but there are common ingredients in happy ones: unconditional love and respect.

Dr. Richard Osibanjo

RICH NUGGETS

Day 341 of 365

The best things in life are free, but they don't last long because it is easier to take them for granted.

Dr. Richard Osibanjo

Day 342 of 365

An inferiority complex mindset is like pouring water into a basket; it never fills up. To keep the water in the basket, you must line it with self-belief.

Dr. Richard Osibanjo

RICH NUGGETS

Leaders must steer clear of making decisions from a limited viewpoint to achieve widespread adoption of their change initiatives. A one-sided account may be true, but it is incomplete. Be intentional in getting 360-degree feedback.

Dr. Richard Osibanjo

Weekly reflection activity

What do these quotes mean to me?

RICH NUGGETS

Day 344 of 365

Patience is a trait we expect from others but forget to give back. Do you need to extend grace to anyone today?

Dr. Richard Osibanjo

Day 345 of 365

You've probably heard the adage, "When in Rome, do as the Romans do." Follow this exceptional guide without compromising your core values.

Dr. Richard Osibanjo

RICH NUGGETS

Day 346 of 365

'Be yourself' is frequently misunderstood. It is not a static state but a journey of discovery and growth.

Dr. Richard Osibanjo

Day 347 of 365

Fever is a symptom, not the root cause of the issue. Dig deeper to uncover the real challenges; your solutions will result in lasting change.

Dr. Richard Osibanjo

RICH NUGGETS

Day 348 of 365

Zelensky, a comedian turned president, became one of the most consequential leaders of our lifetime. Like Zelensky, there is a roar in you: discover, develop, and deliver your gift to the world.

— Dr. Richard Osibanjo

Day 349 of 365

Would I get the same response if I asked ten random people about your organization's key priorities? The fewer diverse responses you receive, the clearer your goals. Why not try out a little experiment?

— Dr. Richard Osibanjo

RICH NUGGETS

Day 350 of 365

Butterfly eggs can take two weeks to several months to metamorphosize. A baby is born after nine months. Apple seeds bear fruit in 5 to 10 years. Your gift determines your incubation period. So, avoid comparing yourself with others.

Dr. Richard Osibanjo

Weekly reflection activity

What can you do today that you didn't think you could do a year ago?

RICH NUGGETS

Day 351 of 365

Look in the mirror if you notice people working around you to get things done.

Dr. Richard Osibanjo

Day 352 of 365

Change happens when leaders create experiences that shift the mindset of their people from compliance to commitment.

Dr. Richard Osibanjo

RICH NUGGETS

Day 353 of 365

To foster collaboration, help your team answer this question, "What value do we create working together that we can't achieve working independently?"

Dr. Richard Osibanjo

Day 354 of 365

Fruits, not seeds, are served on dinner tables. Don't give up if no one is inviting you to the table. Keep watering your seed; your season will come.

Dr. Richard Osibanjo

RICH NUGGETS

Day 355 of 365

Pruning is not a pleasurable experience, but it's essential for a plant to thrive. Similarly, find a tribe of accountability partners to keep you on the path to success.

Dr. Richard Osibanjo

Day 356 of 365

Great leaders are not forged during seasons of abundance. They emerge from the trenches in the off-seasons and uncertain times.

Dr. Richard Osibanjo

RICH NUGGETS

Day 357 of 365

Think of yourself as a product and answer the questions below. What is the purpose of the product? What does it do? Who does it help? How does it work? Where can it be found? What do people say about it?

Dr. Richard Osibanjo

Weekly reflection activity

What can you do today that you didn't think you could do a year ago?

RICH NUGGETS

Day 358 of 365

Software developers send updates and patches to your device to fix bugs and improve performance. Similarly, adopting a growth mindset is how you become a better version of yourself.

Dr. Richard Osibanjo

Day 359 of 365

When it comes to comparison, no one wins. You either believe you are better or fall short. Both are unhealthy. Instead, be content with yourself and aspire to be better than you were yesterday.

Dr. Richard Osibanjo

RICH NUGGETS

Day 360 of 365

It's cheaper and smarter to get insurance before you need it. Use the same strategy when building your network.

Dr. Richard Osibanjo

Day 361 of 365

It's easy to get carried away with other people's success on social media. Remember that grape plants take 2 to 7 years to produce fruit. There are no shortcuts to success; you must put in the work.

Dr. Richard Osibanjo

RICH NUGGETS

Day 362 of 365

At times, the best-kept secrets are in plain sight. No one is coming to your rescue. You are the solution the world is waiting for.

Dr. Richard Osibanjo

Day 363 of 365

To beat the competition, leaders must invest in two types of software. The first is human connection; brains follow hearts. The second is software-centric products and services.

Dr. Richard Osibanjo

RICH NUGGETS

Day 364 of 365

Speed limits are not designed to maximize your car's performance. They protect you and others from harm. The good news is that you are not a car, so don't limit yourself by conforming to other people's expectations.

Dr. Richard Osibanjo

Weekly reflection activity

How do you embrace your authentic self, even if it looks different from what others expect?

RICH NUGGETS

Day 365 of 365

You are the world's best-kept secret. The universe is enormous; to be noticed, you must play big! There is no stopping you now. Go out and bless the world. There is no one like you!

Dr. Richard Osibanjo

Other books by the author

Available on Amazon.com

RICH NUGGETS

A Daily Dose of Inspiration to Jump-start Your Day

Made in the USA
Columbia, SC
23 April 2025